Susan Unterberg

HENRI COLE

THE VISIBLE MAN

Henri Cole was born in Fukuoka, Japan, and was raised in Virginia. The recipient of many awards, including the Kingsley Tufts Poetry Award for his most recent book, *Middle Earth* (FSG, 2003), he is the author of four other books of poetry.

ALSO BY HENRI COLE

Middle Earth (2003)

The Look of Things (1995)

The Zoo Wheel of Knowledge (1989)

The Marble Queen (1986)

THE VISIBLE MAN

THE VISIBLE MAN

HENRI COLE

FARRAR, STRAUS AND GIROUX

NEW YORK

Farrar, Straus and Giroux
19 Union Square West, New York 10003

Copyright © 1998 by Henri Cole
Distributed in Canada by Douglas & McIntyre Ltd.
Printed in the United States of America
Originally published in 1998 by Alfred A. Knopf, Inc.,
a division of Random House, Inc.
Published by Farrar, Straus and Giroux in 2005
First Farrar, Straus and Giroux paperback edition, 2005

Library of Congress Cataloging-in-Publication Data
Cole, Henri.
    The visible man / Henri Cole.— 1st Farrar, Straus and Giroux pbk. ed.
    p. cm.
    ISBN-13: 978-0-374-28448-0 (pbk. : alk. paper)
    ISBN-10: 0-374-28448-2 (pbk. : alk. paper)
    I. Title

PS3553.O4725 V57 2005
811'.6—dc22

                                                2005049459

Designed by Harry Ford

www.fsgbooks.com

1   3   5   7   9   10   8   6   4   2

*For Martin Nugent
and Susan Unterberg*

Yes, I being
the terrible puppet of my dreams, shall
lavish this on you—

HART CRANE, *The Visible the Untrue*

Contents

I

I I

CONTENTS

AUTHOR'S NOTE

For their encouragement, I am indebted to the editors
of the following publications, where poems,
sometimes in different form, were originally published.

THE ATLANTIC MONTHLY: "Horses" and "Childlessness"
THE BOSTON BOOK REVIEW: "Black Mane"
THE NEW ENGLAND REVIEW: "The Black Jacket" and "The Suicide Hours"
THE NEW REPUBLIC: "Jealousy" and "Self-Portrait as Four Styles of Pompeian
    Wall Painting"
THE NEW YORKER: "White Spine" and "Chiffon Morning"
THE PARIS REVIEW: "Anagram," "Charity," "The Color of Feeling and the
    Feeling of Color" and "Apollo"
THE PARTISAN REVIEW: "Folly"
SOUTHWEST REVIEW: "Giallo Antico"
THE THREEPENNY REVIEW: "26 Hands"
THE YALE REVIEW: "Etna"
THE BEST AMERICAN POETRY 1998 *(edited by John Hollander):* "Self-Portrait as
    Four Styles of Pompeian Wall Painting"
MY FAVORITE PLANT *(edited by Jamaica Kincaid):* "Peonies" and "Bearded Irises"

I would also like to record my thanks to the American Academy of Arts and
Letters and the American Academy in Rome, sponsors of the Rome Prize in
Literature, which enabled me to live and travel in Italy during the composi-
tion of much of this book. My thanks also to the Corporation of Yaddo for
hospitality and solitude during valuable residencies.

I

Truth is no Apollo Belvedere, no formal thing.

MARIANNE MOORE, *In the Days of Prismatic Color*

Arte Povera

In the little garden of Villa Sciarra,
I found a decade of poetry dead.
In the limestone fountain lay lizards
and Fanta cans, where Truth once splashed from The Source.

How pleased I was and defiant because
a dry basin meant the end of description & rhyme,
which had nursed and embalmed me at once.
Language was more than a baroque wall-fountain.

Nearby, a gas-light shone its white-hot tongue,
a baby spat up—the stomach's truth-telling—
a mad boy made a scene worthy of Stalin.
Ah, to see the beast shitting in its cage!

Then the lying—"Yes sir, Daddy"—which changes nothing.
My soul-animal prefers the choke-chain.

Self-Portrait as Four Styles of Pompeian Wall Painting

FIRST STYLE

To become oneself is so exhausting
that I am as others have made me,
imitating monumental Greek statuary
despite my own feminized way of being.
Like the empire, I was born of pain—
or like a boy, one might say, for I have
become my father, whom I cannot fathom;
the past is a fetish I disdain.
Since they found the bloodless little girl,
with voluptuous lips, buried in me,
I am unsentimental. I do not see
the gold sky at sunset but blackbirds hurled
like lava stones. I am like a severed
finger lost in the wreckage forever.

SECOND STYLE

Unable to care for people, I care
mostly for things. At my bitterest,
I see love as self-censorship.
My face is a little Roman theater
in perfect perspective—with colonnades
and landscapes—making illusionistic
reference to feelings I cannot admit.
Painted in Dionysiac yellows and reds,
my unconscious is a rocky grotto
where flies buzz like formalists.
Despite myself, I am not a composite
of signs to be deciphered. In the ghetto—
where Jews, prostitutes and sailors once lived—
I am happiest because I am undisguised.

THIRD STYLE

Tearing away at an old self to make
a new one, I am my most Augustan.
I grieve little. I try to accustom
myself to what is un-Hellenized and chaste.
I let my flat black dado assert itself
without ornament. Can it be, at last,
that I am I—accepting lice clasped
to me like a dirty Colosseum cat?
On a faded panel of Pompeian red,
there's an erotic x-ray of my soul:
a pale boy-girl figure is unconsoled,
pinned from behind at the farthest edge
of human love, where the conscience is not whole,
yet finely engraved like a snail's shell.

FOURTH STYLE

If great rooms declare themselves by the life
lived in them, each night I am reborn
as men and boys stroll among the ruins,
anonymously skirting the floodlights,
sinking into me tenderly, as they do
each other during their brief hungry acts.
"As brief as love," they used to say, Plato
and his kind, exiling man from happiness,
but I am more than a cave whose campfire,
swelling and contracting, is all that is real.
Tomorrow, when I am drunk on sunlight,
I will still feel the furtive glances,
the unchaste kisses and the wet skin
imprinting me until I am born again.

White Spine

Liar, I thought, kneeling with the others,
how can He love me and hate what I am?
The dome of St. Peter's shone yellowish
gold, like butter and eggs. *My God,* I prayed
anyhow, as if made in the image
and likeness of Him. Nearby, a handsome
priest looked at me like a stone; I looked back,
not desiring to go it alone.
The college of cardinals wore punitive red.
The white spine waved to me from his white throne.
Being in a place not my own, much less
myself, I climbed out, a beast in a crib.
Somewhere a terrorist rolled a cigarette.
Reason, not faith, would change him.

Folly

In the Doria Pamphili garden,
most of the granite niches are empty,
the male gods have lost their genitals,
and the Great Mother, Hera, has no head.

Something has gone awry
in the artificial lake.
Burrowing deep into the black banks
enclosed by wire mesh,
families of nutria are eradicating—
with webbed hind feet,
blunt muzzled heads
and long orange incisors—
Pope Innocent X's pleasure garden's
eco-system.

       Gothic as the unconscious,
the heavy tapered bodies
root along the irrigation ditches,
making their way in a criminal trot
toward the swans, whose handsome,
ecclesiastical wings open out
obliviously.

Each day I come back.
The sky is Della Robbia blue.
As I rise to my feet,
a swan—immaculate
and self-possessed as the ambulance
bearing my half-dead Mother—
grasps into the depths
and tears a weed up,

dripping like a chandelier,
while paddling behind are the derelict rodents,
hankering—with big sleepy eyes,
suggesting something like matrimonial bliss,
and plush gray fur,
undulating like the coat my mother wore—
to hunt the grass-shrouded
cygnet eggs and gut
their bloody embryos.

Charity

Naked but for dainty shoes, garter
and a ribbon in her long red hair,
she takes him in the way history takes us in:
with an unperturbed hand across the breast.
Stroking into her, the way a boot strokes a stirrup,
he seems as banal or irrelevant
as a birthmark or a hairdo. On screen,
it's her pointy attenuated legs,
smaller than life, that strain to do their work.
What he feels, for good or bad, I cannot feel.
What she feels frees her. Tenderness,
even to a stranger, corroborates the self.
Unlike the pretty jar of libidinal grease
knocked from the bed, she will not break.

The Black Jacket

At the Hunt Club, two architects,
a curator, and I arrived for supper
in palace rooms where a prince once slept.
We'd come to see the frescoes,
though I confess
a crude interest in the titled,
dispossessed of sovereignty or land.

"Tell me," one of the footmen queried
at the gate, "what nation is home?"
Though we wore good tailored suits,
my speech made plain I was not Roman.
Then one of us, in their mother tongue, spoke,
and we were waved to the next station.
If they judged us men without
families or religion, I reasoned,
surely cardinal virtues—strength, justice,
wisdom, moderation—would help us here,
where Bishops mingled with believers.
Yet, on the peristyle, facing us down
without emotion, their chamberlain found
the hound's-tooth jacket worn by James,
a shy farmboy from Napoleon, Ohio,
beneath code, all but black forbidden.
And so with perfect simple manners,
having little to do with class,
he donned the ill-cut garment found for him,
and we were welcomed.

                    In the drawing room,
Europa sat on the broad back of a bull
who lowed and licked her sandaled foot.
Her rape was something not yet accomplished.

Our solemn waiters wore knee-breeches,
tail-coats and shirts with mended lace.
As I cut open the partridge on my plate,
I felt wine in my veins like scorched silk.

Years ago I stood in line with others,
hands polished as a case of knives,
serving senators and their pretty wives,
who chewed on baby lamb and looked at me
but saw no swimmer rising from the deep:
I was not me. History, its white teeth
jammed with gristle, had not yet set me free.

Unlike dear James, the architect of rooms,
who would choose to dismantle them
rather than conform,
who said nothing
while swallowing the hot forkfuls.
As he scratched the collar
of his borrowed coat,
his eyes were watering.
A little puddle of pink lamb juice
seemed to be admonishing him
for progeny that would not be.
From a lintel, a leopard gazed at us.
Something pricked us like a saw:
captivity was breeding consciousness.

In the carpark,
James came back to us
wearing his Sunday best.
Dirty gravel scraped my polished black boots.
Someone remarked on the blue bougainvillea—
nailed up like Christ.
Somewhere a she-wolf suckled the young,
who would hunt each other.

The Scholars

In the elegant prison,
most of the time, like an elephant,
I feel immovable and alone.

Day & night,
beauty is a scorned thing and is not everlasting.
Fragments of statuary ornament the cortile,
like bodies sinking in quicksand.
Even a luckless prick
is frozen in the stucco.
Room unfolds into room, gleaming white.
High-heels crisscross the parquet,
assaulting contemplation
like hail battering wheat.
Do not mention little boys trained as "minnows"
to lick and nibble Tiberius
when he went swimming.
Do not mention Cleopatra,
reprehensible because she was
neither madonna nor whore.
Never mind that might begets fear, which orphans us.
Never mind that the weak do not inherit the earth.
Like cultists drinking from a vial,
a new generation is pledging itself to a past,
which is not, they say, inchoate,
and to a world, which is not,
they say, primal:

        no war's sound is heard.
So we speak often of good Augustus,
instead of blood, hate & hunger.
At dinner a cat with a tragic mouth—

like drowned Antinoüs—strokes our calves,
pawing scraps of meat we throw at it.
Our high-sounding debate of Modernism and Marx
is derivative and indiscriminate.
Why do we even bother,
since everything post-Christianity,
post-Constantine, is regarded with dismay?
On the lawn we play croquet,

                              slamming each other's balls
through tired wickets. I, Janus-faced,
can see that the grass is groomed like a cemetery's.
Sublime umbrella pines and proud cypresses
remind us of two ways of being:
why do we choose the cypresses,
so rigid and self-possessed?
Of course, all men want to be strong;
but must their minds, buried in scrolls,
making little hatchet strokes,
be so disengaged from their bodies?

They grow old in their studies,
with bony thighs and baggy stomachs,
reading languages that are countryless,
revising history & art with a lens
that is cracked like the empire.
Jasmine sprays the air,
the same to them as cigarette smoke.
A baby Hercules wrestles a serpent in the fountain,
but it too is uncataclysmic.
They envy nobody and nothing.
They eat big bowls of pasta
and drain their preposterous bowels.
Out there, it is Sunday
in the country of our origin.

As the sun goes down,
a vast palette of edifices
is changing travertine into Vatican gold.
Listen to the swallows capsizing in a pink sky
folding over the gated prison.

Etna

Who are you, whose pornographic voice
and little surreptitious breaths
are meant to taunt me,
again and again, at home on tape?
Who are you, whose straining tumescence
and plundering come-cries
make a man a mule?
Are your white teeth showing?
Are your pectorals waxed like a prostitute's?
Are your taut thighs spread like a dead man's?

Hearing your exhortations,
I feel invisible and gritty and cold
as when I hiked a long volcano slope,
feet snow-soaked, eyes prismatic.
It was Easter Monday,
something gathered and broke.
A hand stroked the back of my neck:
it was mine, smeared with sweat.
White smoke radiated everywhere.
White ice chopped underfoot.
I glimpsed myself, reddish like an ant,
crisscrossing the lapilli,
twisted like rope.
Goodbye, I said to God's looming hand.
Air: Easter lily bright.
Goodbye, to false art, evading life.
Fire: I coughed asthmatically.
Goodbye, to the Sodomite's self-loathing.
At last, *Earth* was pollinating me,
with my curly white hairs and aging belly.
More: I rubbed mineral *Water* on my face.

Stranger, with genitalia greased,
whose "brotherly love" can be bought or sold,
whose avaricious body disdains the effeminate,
I have been waiting for you.
Come, unlace my boots; I chose you.

To a Prince

At the sound of your name, I turned my head.
How does it feel
to meet a man and know he'll acquiesce?

You make no avowals
because you cannot keep them;
your only worship is that monolith,
the patrician past—
you, whose nocturnal addiction is flesh,
you, with whom I streaked through Rome
on a motorino.

I want the external world
to continue the interior monologue of who I am:
hence, the narrow mattress under me,
with sinking springs,
symbolizes solitude,
instead of my inferior class.
Ensconced in your period rooms of white and gold,
you couldn't care less. What a pity
you cannot kiss yourself.

In the steamroom,
where there is no moral order
and secret emotions channel themselves
toward the idolized body,
I could see the back of you,
lowering your head to a cock,
brown as a speckled egg.

If it's true you're marrying,
be kind to her. Public lies sow the seeds
of private shame. Yours and hers.

Giallo Antico

*On August 5th, commemorating a miracle
of the Virgin, white feathers simulating
snow are released from the ceiling of
Santa Maria Maggiore in Rome.*

None of the indolent Christians could see
the small brown hand in a coffer of the ceiling
throwing white feathers into the nave.
Everything extraneous preoccupied them,
brought to their knees, like little worn machines of Christ,
by a simulation of falling snow
against plundered gold.
That was the story.
                I held my tongue,
not seeing the ornamental roses three feet wide,
not seeing the Virgin dressed like an Oriental empress,
admiring, instead, thirty-six marble pillars;
I tried not to think of faith as something given up,
like freedom, to an invisible Master.
But how sad they looked, on their knees like praying figurines,
flecked with snow.
What God could make such a fetish
of their pain & suffering?
Why did they not strike back?

                         Still worse,
preceding centuries unfolded.
I saw a work camp, a North African quarry,
slaves, many of them exiled Christians,
like subterranean hordes of rats,
moving blocks on a road to Carthage,
yellow marble columns for a basilica in Rome.
Giallo antico slabs, dishes, pestles and mortars:

after heavy rain, they emerge from the soil
inside the flooded prison walls,
where archeologists are digging,
all that is left of a God
who is Master of Pain because he is not human.

The Color of Feeling
and the Feeling of Color

While others were discussing
the styles of metopes,
I lay down in the Temple of Zeus
and shut my eyes.

       Behind the shut eyes,
the metopes were what I saw:
a giant tugged on the arrow in his head;
a son's corpse wasted on a funeral bed;
a centaur crashed into a pit;
a wrestler cut off his head to honor his father;
and everywhere were grieving women,
tearing at their hair.

           It might almost have been a lion
grazing among the war-dead
that licked the flesh of my forehead,
though it was only a bearded dog.
It was midday, and a church bell
wagged its lead tongue furiously at us,
making one think of life-in-death and all that.
Overhead, a Hades crow split the sky.
Water buffalo roamed the desolate farmland,
holding their shoulders proudly like invaders,
yet grunting in their miserable
tamed beast fashion.

        All those centuries
of vengeance and maw, recapped in an hour,
clung to the mind like marble dust.
The nerves sat crumbling

like opus reticulatum—
little tufa blocks piled in a phalanx,
lantern-lit at the end of the tunnel.
But when I looked up in front of me,
into a shaft of fresh, clean light,
fourteen limestone columns
rose to their doric entablature,
as if to say austerely, "Wake up!
This is the house of Zeus.
So much anguish demeans the gods."

Then I saw a little Apollonian room,
the zone of art,
asserting itself as a cure.
"Beauty is not structure,"
it seemed to say, rebuking me,
"but structure & carnage,
hurting and consoling us at once.
Neither one subordinates the other."
This was not so long ago,
in a country, many rivers and realms away,
where rooms were *stanze*,
patterns of words tethering the mind
in endless motions.

         But it was time to move on.
Our guide beckoned us from the rubble,
where the temple stood serene as Zeus.
I wiped the bitter saliva from my brow.
Far off, a lemon grove traced
the slope of a volcano,
a dolphin cut the sea.

(*Paestum, 1995*)

The Blue Grotto

Curlyhead was bellowing Puccini
and making the boat rock.
The sun shone like a Majolica clock.
The sea boiled noisily.
I lay down like a child in a box.
It was my birthday.

                          Above, on a cliff,
a mule pissed on us.
Then the dragging chain
as we lurched into the chasm.
Archaic cooings: Byzantine blue.
J removed her tortoiseshell glasses,
crossing her pretty legs.
C thoughtfully stroked his goatee.
I sat up, as in a coffin
after three hundred lovers.
Starboard, an oar-blade splashed
emeralds against valedictory black.
Once again, description,
unemotional shorthand
for sublimated wisdom,
fails to conjure what we felt;
the poem yearns for something more.
Like me: childless.
My love & I: gutted words.
My prick: like an instrument for an altar
or surgeon's table,
shiny & maleficent.

Stalactites,
like jaws, bedeviled us.
Sunlight struck the sandy bottom:
Giotto blue, the Tennessean said;
Florida blue, the tobacco queen said;
Cognitive blue, I, the unanalyzed, said.
Nothing from Curlyhead, who rowed vigorously.
Then a serpentine thing,
with five pairs of legs grasping at us,
appeared beside our little boat,
unidentifiably damaged,

as the young man was,
who boarded our bus going home.
His arms flailed spasmodically.
His face was pinched like a retarded boy's.
I dedicate this poem to him,
whose unneediness shamed me,
demanding I acknowledge the best in myself,
whose arms & legs
racked the blue lapidary air,
as if burdened by ropes, lantern, & pick,
while he bantered brilliantly to himself,
the mind struggling
to overcome the stick that is the body.

Painted Eyes

Dusty and treeless, the street sloped beneath us.
Somewhere a hammer made thunderclaps,
forging the night-sky.

Then the children,
seeing us, dashed from the Moorish houses,
vigorously shouting, vying for position,
while the bravest,
in worn underpants and plastic sandals,
climbed a high crater-like wall
and plunged, with murderous cries,
into the Roman pool
where blue-lipped fish waited.
Ah, those glorious soaked heads, spiked like palm fronds!
Seeing one in our group clutch her purse—
repelled by the wet black princes
who shivered in circles of yellow mud
and begged from us—
I felt ashamed.
In the brief African twilight,
a canary chirped something
shrewdly about avarice.

Far off, in the little neighborhood
where I grew—with neat cement walkways
and crab-apple blossoms—
money ran through the fingers
of our house, with nothing much
to record its loss but unhappiness:
one of us ironing servilely,
one of us sobbing in a bedroom,
one of us sleeping on a rifle,

one of us seizing another by the hair,
demanding the animal-like submission
we thought was love.

                    Sunday evening.
Mother is wearing a big cotton shift
and tweezing her eyebrows.
Her head is a thicket of hairpins.
In the round hand-mirror
that parodies her face,
the world looks greater than it is.
I am next to bathe in the water
of the poor earth, reused by each of us
in order of birth. Gray with sodium and grit,
it covers me like a black robe,
and yet I feel exalted.

                   Soon the violent rain,
like wet Sahara sand, would fall,
scrubbing the hot labyrinthine
corridors of shuttered houses and aimless dogs,
where the sparse life is
purgative and inexhaustible,
where little pilfering hands
moved freely in and out
of my trouser pockets,
though there were no diamonds
except those the eyes mined.

Adam Dying

(Piero della Francesca, The Story of Adam. Arezzo, San Francesco)

Though the most we can say is that it is
as if there was a world before Adam,
even that seems narrow and parochial
as we contemplate his dying . . . while Eve,
with withered breasts, watches pensively,
and the mellifluous young, in animal skins,
stand about emotionless, like pottery.
What do the significant glances mean?

Can only Adam—naked, decrepit,
sprawled in the dirt—see what dying is?
How can they not hear the moaning, smell the body,
suffer the burden of original sin?
East & West, armies revile each other.
Mothers hunt among the decomposing dead.

26 Hands

Thus are we when gathering together
to contemplate the unthinkable:
somber & a little run-down.
At their long table
laid out in a white cloth,
so much fealty between brothers
looks, at first, sentimental or false.
Then the speaking hands pull a belt
around the unbeliever's heart:

                          Doubting Thomas
shakes his finger in the air.
"Put your finger here, Thomas,"
Christ will say in a few days' time,
showing him the nail holes.
Somnolent John, the faithful one,
with no chest to lay his head upon,
folds his hands serenely.
Poor Peter grasps a knife prophetically;
later, he'll cut off a soldier's ear.
They, in turn, will crucify him, upside-down.
Impetuous James, the older one, is blocking
the others with outstretched arms,
as the younger one, with an open face like Jesus',
reaches out to touch Peter's shoulder.
But it is too late.

Isolated, with heavy arms
and a fist of money,
the one who will change us all
has upset the salt shaker,
portending more bad luck.

Bartholomew, in whom there is no falseness,
rises and puts his big hands flat on the table.
Sweet Philip points to himself almost femininely,
asking, "Could it be me?"
With open palms before him,
Andrew tries to calm them.
Handsome Matthew cannot take in what is happening;
his long manicured hands betray his wealth.
All the light from the window
shines on Simon's bald head
as he gestures thoughtfully to Thaddeus,
who is looking right at me
and wringing his hands,
as if to ask, "Do you believe?"
But it is too late.

        Great folds of silk,
patterned with hoo birds and yellow dragons,
arrive under parasols out of the rain.
Thirteen kimonos,
each one spotlit like a paradigm,
pass demurely into the refectory.
With medallions tinkling on their black wigs
and thick swathed obis tied much too tight,
standing face to face with the apostles,
woman to man, what do they see?

        Art:
the oldest thing on Earth, touched up,
bombed, vanishing beneath excrement
of large and small organisms.
Human anguish: Buddhist or Catholic,
it deadens us. Betrayal:
that lead coffin among wooden coffins.
Supper: pewter plates heaped with lamb bones,

a glass of wine (not spilt blood),
hunks of bread (not flesh).
Jesus: who cannot lead us all.
Sunset: bathing humanity sympathetically,
despite the muddling.
And forgiveness: sentimental manna
so hard to swallow it unshackles us.

II

And, if the soul is about to know itself, it must gaze into the soul.

PLATO, Alcibiades

Childlessness

For many years I wanted a child
though I knew it would only illuminate life
for a time, like a star on a tree; I believed
that happiness would at last assert itself,
like a bird in a dirty cage, calling me,
ambassador of flesh, out of the rough
locked ward of sex.

          Outstretched on my spool-bed,
I am like a groom, alternately seeking fusion
with another and resisting engulfment by it.
A son's love for his mother is like a river
dividing the continent to reach the sea:
I believed that once. When you died, Mother,
I was alone at last. And then you came back,
dismal and greedy like the sea, to reclaim me.

Chiffon Morning

I am lying in bed with my mother,
where my father seldom lay. Little poem,
help me to say all I need to say, better.
Hair dyed, combed; nails polished; necklace-like scar
ear-to-ear; stocky peasant's bulk hidden
under an unfeminine nightgown; sour-milk
breaths rehearsing death, she faces me, her room
a pill museum where orange teabags
draining on napkins almost pass for art.
Even the Christmas amaryllis sags
under the weight of its blood red
petals, unfolding like a handkerchief.
From the television screen, a beauty-
pageant queen waves serenely at me.

II

In the oily black barbecue smoke,
in our blue Chevrolet station wagon,
in a cottage at the sea, no one spoke
but me to the nerveless God
who never once stopped their loveless act:
the cursing mouths, the shoving and choking,
the violent pulse, the wrecked hair, the hunchbacked
reprisal, the suddenly inverted sky,
the fiendish gasping, the blade that cuts all
understanding, the white knuckles, the fly
remarkably poised on a blue throat.
I try to pity them. Perhaps God did
on those occasions when battle was a prelude
to sex, and peace, like an arrow, found us.

III

How many nights did I throw my arms around
our black dog's neck and listen to Mother,
on her knees, retching supper? The love hound
licked my face again and again like fur.
Far off, the weirdly ethereal bells
of an ice cream truck, hypnotic in contrast,
calmed me like tapers burning steadily.
Near dawn, when she was pregnant with her last-
born, there were complications. The long path
to the ambulance was splashed with what came
from inside her, a floating purplish wax
our neighbor, a cheerful woman, mopped up.
When Mother came home thin again, the sun crowned
whom she cradled. Father was out of town.

IV

On the mowed grass, I once posed in black tie;
now a neighbor's labradors sow lawn-burn.
Pink dogwoods Mother and I transplanted
throw off their sentimental silks.
If squirrels nest in a tree too close by,
she hires a colonel's son to oust them.
No one calls except born-again women.
"Must you tell everyone what you are?"
she protests, during each of our visits;
I rake leaves and burn them like a corpse,
wondering if I'm better off without her—
like Father when he was a GI
and their trailer-park love got coffined up
in a suburban dream house, for sale now.

V

As the cuckoo clock crows in the kitchen,
on her nightstand others as bluntly chime,
but cannot break her drugged oblivion.
Please wake up, Mother, and wet your cottonmouth.
"She was agitated," nurses whispered
when we found her tied to the bed, knocked out.
Demerol blocked the pain, entering through the eyes,
while the mind, crushed like a wineglass, healed.
"I'll bury you all," she gloated, at home again.
Months later, they stitched her throat in surgery.
The voice that had been on the radio
when the war was on, plunged a tragic octave.
More pills crowded her daily glass of milk.
My guilt seemed vain compared to what she felt.

VI

Mother is naked and holding me up
above her as soap streams from my face
(I'm wearing a dumb ape's frown) into the tub
where she is seated: the mind replays
what nurtures it. The black months when she
would lie assassinated like our Siamese cat
are still far off. Yet, tranced by a lush light,
which no one else sees, like a leaden bee
shackled to a poppy, I am not free.
Each time I am dunked in the green, green
sacramental water, I glare shamelessly
as she shrieks and kisses me, gripped in air;
I do not know if she loves me or cares,
if it's suffering or joy behind her tears.

The Coastguard Station

At dawn, a few recruits have a smoke
on the patio above the breakers;
across the sand path, I sit with my books,
hearing their animal coughs.

Strangely, watching them tranquillizes me.
Their big clapboard house
is illuminated all night,
like the unconscious, though no one enters.
Even in hallucinatory fog,
their pier is flash-bulb bright
and staunch as Abraham.
Overhead, a gull scavenges like a bare hand.
An officer, in orange overalls,
stares like a python
up into the window where I am.

What does it mean to be chosen?
To have your body grow into a hero's
and have done nothing to achieve it?
To seize a birthright, unobstructed?
To dominate with confident bearing?
That is their covenant,
even cold-stupefied and lethargic:
hearing the blessing of Isaac to Jacob.
Naked and a little drunk,
I sit chafing at it,
the nerves in my teeth aching,
lording it over the rest of me.

Why do I appear to be what I am not?
To the world, arrogantly self-sufficient.

To myself, womanish, conflicted, subservient,
like Esau pleading, "Bless me also, Father!"
I hate what I am and I hate what I am not.

Anagram

Thy word is all, if we could spell.
GEORGE HERBERT, *The Flower*

Scrawling the letters of my name,
I found and changed what I became:

first, HERON LICE emerged,
like shame usurping dignity.

Then LION CHEER assembled,
as if proof I was palimpsest.

When the strange oracle decreed,
"OH, RECLINE," I went deep

into the core of my being,
where I found LICHEN ROE,

something called IRON LEECH—germs
to help a man plough up himself.

Then the musings got profane.
"I CLONE HER!" the voice sneered,

speaking of Mother;
and there's LICE ON HER.

But I was scribe. No!
I shouted, I NO LECHER.

I am not an ECHO LINER.
I was I. So self-love came back,

replacing alphabetical tears.
Little parts of me COHEREd:

CORN, RICE & EEL.
All I was I could feel.

Horses

Setting out on my bicycle alone,
I came upon the horses
drenched in bright sunshine,
yard after yard of blue-black ironed silk,
drawn before stopped traffic.

With white stars on their foreheads
and white bracelets on their legs,
each blood horse wore nothing
but a fine noseband
and a shroud of steam.

I felt lazy and vicious watching them,
with my large joints and big head,
stricken by thoughts of my brothers.
If only the barbarous horsemen
could lead *us* down the path, unestranged.

It smashed in me like water galloped through.
Flinching there on my haunches,
with wide nostrils,
nipping the air as if it were green grass,
how I yearned for my neck to be brushed!

Colloquy

All night I have slept by you.
A fan makes the sound of a river.

Ah, how easily my arrogance is broken.

I am older than you
and enthralled
by your candied tongue
as you
yank the buckle around my waist.

Across the parquet,
one solitary black ant
transports another,
like a soldier,
over its head.

Darling, have I been too harsh?

Farther,
you say.

And so
we sink deeper,
like drowned men, into the river
that converts our bedsheets
into a shroud.

When the river, like a body, speaks,
"In me thou must float,"

why do I know I must go
into the great etherizing crests?

*

Sometimes I cannot look at your face.

Faced by you,
I am nobody,
except the one who comes,
dragging my heart,
my pony, across the city,
where you lie breathing in the dark.

In the mirror,
little creases meet
at the corner of my eyes.
My horsy soul has a hard mouth with sharp teeth.
Impertinent brown curls
creep up around my neck.

But you are younger
and make me feel
unfalsified,
instead of what I am.

Unlike adulterers, we are not hurting others,
you argue.

Yet everything you command I do—
your gentleman seducer,
in a small white room with white bedding,
where there are fleecy entangled limbs,
and blood-smell
and locked terrestrial mouths—

I fear it is consuming us,
like moths singed by flame.

The White Marriages

Some days the white marriage has a black face.
Braiding the cornrows around her scalp,
I know I am a lucky man.
The black telephone rings frustrated as a hard cock,
because she is wholly focused on me.
When she twists her long legs in a parody of desire,
I don't know what makes me feel so free,
unless it's intimacy.
And I don't know what we'll become.
Orient pearls at her ears glisten
like the bright white man and wife we are not.

Other days the white marriage has the face
of a camera, not pointed at me, but at us together,
looking out, usually at art:
                                        I'm the cynical one.
She's more affectionate. She holds the camera.
"Look, can't you just be you?" she implores,
faithful as a wife.
Because two people falling in love
have everything to lose and nothing to gain,
what we give each other is not
helpless limb-wrapping climaxes,
I confess, but empathy, acid-bit
by truth, that highly discriminating love
that needs no body.

The Long View

What I fear most are ordinary things:
poverty, alcoholism, lovelessness.
But these are not what preoccupy me,
come night, when I sit in my rooms and sweat,
often with such high-caffeinated self-pity,
I must turn to Him for help.
Withdrawn and muttering, I cannot face
even the plainest facts of my life alone.
Not to speak of the little shame-filled list,
accreting like a tumor in my head:
being stood up at the opera;
a forgotten birthday; a trick's backtalk—
"I wasn' doin' nothin', Bitch!";
unpaid debts; slamming doors; technicolor lies.
So much of it bile to the self.
                              And yet,
sometimes, when I turn to the crucifix,
all I see is a naked man, wounded,
utterly desirable, hanging on my wall.

Without God, I am able to accept
every sin, every compulsion,
like the sting of peroxide on cut flesh.
With my cabbage-green eyes,
I look beyond the jaundiced past,
beyond the doctrine of the Fall,
the *Felix Culpa* and all that,
to the long view that laminates a life,
to the untheatrical terminus in a chair,
a kind of protean human surrogate,
upholding me with arms & legs, back & seat,
made of bronze or Adirondack branches, I do not care.

Mesmerism

I

Long afterward, people would say blandly,
"Those boys might have done something with their lives."
My suffering didn't frighten them.
I was only a stereotype, waiting
in the snow like a rabbit, asking for life.
It wasn't who but what I was their sons
did not understand as one tethered
my hands behind my head with my necktie.
Weirdly, the pain was comforting—"Take it!"
I thought, "I wish I could give you more"—letting
me know I was alive before I would die.
This was not nobility. I pissed on myself,
groaning aloud, wanting the face
of the sweaty boy who strangled me.

II

Everyone wants to die without pain.
Kneeling before us, with his pretty mouth,
he was a prototype of innocence.
Sweet Jesus, I wanted to hit him. So we did.
Each blow taking us farther than we'd been.
With his neck pulled back, showing the soft front,
and half-naked slender legs, he made me sick.
"I want! I want!" I kept hearing in my head,
without understanding how I was governed
by the thing I'd hated. "I'm just like you,"
he moaned, "I have a mother," which made us laugh.
After the punishment, he lay supine,
as on a china platter. My teeth were foaming.
All that I am was membrane and nails.

The Suicide Hours

Ignorant and unabashed, I sit in a tub of gas,
cherishing nothing and nobody.

My head, that well-fed lamb,
cannot even find you, O God, whom I loved.

My flesh is the flesh of a single man:
mutable, corrupt.

I do not believe in "like mother like son."
I do not believe life is art, undone.

I do not believe in the orange poppies,
odorless as wax. Cheated and sucked dry,

I believe in nothing, except the wooden match,
thrown like my blue daddy's neck-cross,

into the bath where faith, hope, & charity
toss against spent semen, saliva, & tears.

Jealousy

I, putative poet, I,
with goat ears alert
and chewed up nails
and hirsute back,
I, with Judas eyes averted,
moaning like a sluttish dove, I,
with numb lips and tight throat,
believing hope
is a shallow man's illusion—
is this my portent of Hell?
Mine, the cottage, heaped with roses, by the sea.
Mine, the ill-behaved boys rifling the life.
Mine, the fame, that demi-god, subordinating me.
The imagination, like a milk bucket,
is filled with dung—
is this my altar-shrine?
Something is biting me over the eye, drawing blood.
My scrotum dangles like a street dog's.
Self-esteem, like herringbone pavement,
is breaking up in cartfuls.
Where is the comfort of pears on a window ledge?
To be alone is to be a stranger.
I am he.
This is my autopsy.

Black Mane

Do you hear him, how he's asking?
Say something to him.
Let him feel your presence.

When he paws the ground, lies down and rolls luxuriously,
when he stands up, shakes the dust off and snorts vigorously,
do not stand in his shadow.
Go to him. Grasp his mane,
like the handle of a coffin, and climb on.
Don't worry, he will be patient with you,
who fell ill as a child from the feel
of not feeling anything,
who were nourished on violent adult fare.
He sees you laid bare riding him,
following his head like a lovesick pupil.
He knows you will not raise your crop to him.
He feels your flesh twitching against his.

At last you have what you have longed for,
as if man on a horse constituted a single creature,
like a man on a high rock
at the edge of a field.
But now, the creature leaps about the field,
the self is not a lonely figure in the sun.
The days when you lay his reins in a loop on his withers
and stand beside him, groping his neck,
if he lays back his ears and bares his teeth,
do not feel unworthy.
Body & soul cannot always
be alive together.

           With him, a commandment will be broken:
walk, trot, stop, turn—these are only words

and yet he obeys them, obedient and calm.
His surrender is not a servile thing.
His power is born not of muscle and blood,
but of a self, like a monument
excavated in the sun.
Feel how your soul burns hard
and is changed by him?
See how he fears and respects you
without fact or reason?
See him looking straight ahead
as if it were Hadrian on his back?
Rub molasses on his bit
and he'll fling his heels in a capriole.

When your body sorrows into his,
it is as if a bolt is pushed into place,
metal hitting metal, like wisdom.
And his body, bridled and saddled, conveying yours
brings nothing like grace or redemption,
those taming biblical things,
but like a wave, like a loud chord, like a masterpiece
of oiled canvas, it brings a pulsing, an incessant ravening,
like a robin pouncing at a worm, that nurses
the individuated being, like a tight bud,
into something unsparing while blooming,
and electric, like a paddock fence,
making all that is contained within it
aware of all that is not,
as ash in an urn
must remember the flesh it once was.

Peonies

Ample creamy heads beaten down vulgarly,
as if by some deeply sado-masochistic impulse,
like the desire to subdue, which is normal and active,
and the desire for suffering, which is not;
papery white featherings stapled to long stalks,
sopped with rain and thrown about violently,
as Paul was from his horse by the voice of Christ,
as those he judged & condemned were, leaving the earth;
and, deeper in, tight little buds that seem to blush
from the pleasure they take in being submissive,
because absolute humility in the face of cruelty
is the Passive's way of becoming himself;
the groan of it all, like a penetrated body—
those of us who hear it know the feeling.

Bearded Irises

I was a stranger and you welcomed me.
I thought: he will not stand for the stench of my body.
But truth is a bright needle pulling an ugly thread
and he opened his arms to take me in.
I thought: I love this ordinary man who is made
of the best intentions.
I thought: here's a man who will keep his promise.
In the bars, I was a doomed and lovely thing,
like a flower doomed by frost,
but now I have been redeemed.
I was thirsty and you gave me your glass.
I thought: he will be disgusted seeing wine
run into my open mouth, making my teeth shiver.
But it was dusk and the somber blue sky
began melting like an iris,
abstracting him into its fading light.
I was hungry and you gave me meat.
Eating vigorously with my hands,
I thought: I am like a bearded iris,
my ego unsubjugated.
I demand and get a bed of my own,
from which the whole world of the Not-Me
seems fatal and ridiculous.
I was naked and you clothed me.
I thought: he'll not let me wear his handsome red coat.
To different men come different blessings.
This was a coat worthy of Cocteau.
But you made me put it on.
I thought: now, I am like a red boat,
blazing on a lake.
I was sick and you comforted me.
How I awaited your visits, as a caged dog awaits liberation,

your face—sculpted with little crow's feet,
the mark of a man with an interior life—
healing me like the sun.
If I were in prison you would defend me.
I would think: one day soon I'll be home again.
I would think: how precious silver is
stolen from a man with a great estate,
a man I hate!
And when I die, you will bury me,
easing my corpse into the sepulcher,
as a rotting iris is plunged into compost.
A bare bulb at the center of the vault
will illuminate your face,
and I will think: nothing that comes after
could be as good as what came before.

Apollo

O let me clean my spirit of all doubt,
Give me the signature of what I am.

OVID, *The Metamorphoses*, II

I

With a shriek gulls fled across a black sky,
all of us under the pier were silent,
my blood ached from waiting, then we resumed.
"You're just like us," some bastard said;
and it was true: my hair was close-cropped,
my frame reposed against a piling, my teeth
glistened, my prick was stiff. Little by little
they had made me like them, raptly feeding
in silhouette, with exposed abdomen,
like a spider sating itself. For a moment,
I was the eye through which the universe
beheld itself, like God. And then I gagged,
stumbling through brute shadows to take a piss,
a fly investigating my wet face.

II

Stay married, God said. One marriage.
      Don't abortion. Ugly mortal sin.
Beautiful gorgeous Mary loves you
      so much. Heaven tremendous thrill
of ecstasy forever. What you are,
      they once was, God said, the beloved ones
before you; what they are, you will be.
      All the days. Don't fornicate. Pray be good.
Serpent belly thorn and dust. Serpent belly
      sing lullaby. Beautiful gorgeous Jesus
loves you so much. Only way to Heaven
      church on Sunday. You must pray rosary.
Toil in fields. Heaven tremendous thrill
      of ecstasy forever. Don't fornicate.

III

hefting me onto him
he let me cling on
like a little bear
my ardor my enemy
my cold legs clenching
the hard hairy chest
that was his body
middle-aged floating
under me until
a wall of salt
took us down
in a good clean break
I could feel like a stump
where love had been

IV

The search for a single dominan⁺ gene—
"the 'O-God' hypothesis" (one-gene,
one disorder)—which, like an oracle,
foreknows the sexual brain, is fruitless.

The human self is undeconstructable
montage, is poverty, learning, & war,
is DNA, words, is acts in a bucket,
is agony and love on a wheel that sparkles,

is a mother and father creating
and destroying, is mutable
and one with God, is man and wife speaking,
is innocence betrayed by justice,

is not sentimental but sentimentalized,
is a body contained by something bodiless.

V

"Knowledge enormous makes a God of me,"
Apollo cried, square-shouldered, naked, hair falling
down his back. Now that I am forty, nothing
I have learned proves this. Inside my chest
there is loose straw. Inside my brain there are
syllables and sound. Living inwardly,
how can I tell what is real and what is not?

Joy and grief pulse like water from a fountain
over me, a stone, but do not end as knowledge.
All my life, doing things in moderation,
I have wooed him, whose extremes are forgotten,
whose battered faceless torso fills me
with longing and shame. I lie in the grass
like a man whose being has miscarried.

VI

On the sand there were dead things from the deep.
Faint-lipped shells appeared and disappeared,
like language assembling out of gray.

Then a seal muscled through the surf,
like a fetus, and squatted on a sewage pipe.
I knelt in the tall grass and grinned at it.

Body and self were one, vaguely
coaxed onward by the monotonous waves,
recording like compound sentences.

The seal was on its way somewhere cold, far.
Nothing about it exceeded what it was
(unlike a soul reversing itself to be

something more or a pen scratching words
on vellum after inking out what came before).

VII

Dirt so fine it is like flour.
                       Dirt mixed with ice.
Huge expanses of it.
                 The ground frozen.
With deep exceptional holes.
                      This is what I see
spilling down a nave.
               Then Daddy kissing
a cardinal's ring.
             And the long black snake
of his belt yanked
               around him. His legs
planted apart like a clergyman's.
                  My body
prostrate on the counterpane
              where man and wife lay.
The inflamed buttocks.
              The Roman letters,
TU ES PETRUS,
         though I knew I was not.
Daddy's voice moving slowly,
             like a cancer
toward the brain,
         a sky-blue globe
it cannot penetrate.
              Leather flying against flesh.
In the mouth
        dirt so fine it is like flour.

VIII

Walking in woods, I found him bound to a tree,
moaning like a dove, a kerchief stopping his mouth;
a sweat-smell mixed with mulch and lotion,
a ten dollar bill at his dirty feet.
How easily in him I could see myself,
poor wannabe Sebastian, sucked and bitten
like a whore! I blushed for him, hurrying home.

Memory: the diplomats in white tie
stepping from a Mercedes at the Vatican.
The limousine door swung wide like a gate
to a realm I wanted, a way of being,
formal as Bernini's rigid colonnade.
Then purple-sashed bishops flooded the square,
smearing out the white surplices of acolytes.

IX

All I want is to trust a man with plain
unshaken faith. Because I was not loved,
I cannot love. Sometimes I think I am not alive
but frozen like debris in molten glass.
White hairs sprout from my ears like a donkey's.
I do not feel sorry so much as weak,
like a flower with a broken stem.
A little blood or forgiveness does not
improve things. My brain is staunch as a crow,
my tongue buoyant as a dolphin. Yet, I
do not grow. You, with your unfalse nature
and silver arrows, won't you take my wrist.
Speak to me. My words are sounds
and sounds are not what I feel. Make me a man.

X

To write what is human, not escapist:
that is the problem of the hand moving
apart from my body.
       Yet, subject is
only pretext for assembling the words
whose real story is process is flow.
So the hand lurches forward, gliding back
serenely, radiant with tears, a million
beings and objects hypnotizing me
as I sit and stare.
       Not stupefied. Not aching.
Today, I am one. The hand jauntily
at home with evil, with unexamined feelings,
with just the facts.
       Mind and body, like spikes,
like love and hate, recede pleasantly.
Do not be anxious. The hand remembers them.

XI

When I was a boy our father cooked
to seek forgiveness for making our house
a theater of hysteria and despair.
How could I not eat gluttonously?

You, my Apollo, cannot see that your hands
moving over me, the plainer one,
make me doubt you, that a son's life is punishment
for a father's. Young and penniless,

you serve me lobster. Scalding in the pot,
how it shrieked as I would with nothing left!
Please forgive my little dramas of the self.
And you do . . . in an interruption of the night,

when one body falls against another—
in the endless dragging of chains that signifies love.

XII

Morning of Puritans. Ice on the pond.
Giblets boiling. Any sort of movement
makes the bluejays fly. Father's door is opening.
Why are the titmice so unafraid of him?
Wrapped in cellophane on a granite slab,
the iced heart of our turkey stops time.

I remember my life in still pictures
that fall, inflamed, as in the seventh circle
the burning rain prevents the sodomites
from standing still. But I am in motion,
stroking toward what I cannot see, like an oar
dipped into the blood that ravishes it,

until blood-sprays rouse the dissolute mind,
the ineffable tongue arouses itself.

XIII   CYPARISSUS

"I am here. I will always succor you,"
he used to say, a little full of himself.
What did I know, I was just a boy
loved by Apollo. There had been others.
All I wanted was to ride my deer,
who made me feel some knowledge of myself,
letting me string his big antlers with violets.

One day, in a covert, not seeing the deer
stray to drink at a cool spring, I thrust
my spear inadvertently into him.
Not even Apollo could stop the grief,
which gave me a greenish tint, twisting my
forehead upward; I became a cypress.
Poor Apollo: nothing he loves can live.

XIV

This is not a poem of resurrection.
The body secretes its juices and then is gone.
This is a poem of insurrection
against the self. In the beginning was the child,
fixating on the mother, taking himself
as the sexual object. . . . You know the story.
In the mirror I see a man with a firm
masculine body. Mouth open like a fish,
I look at him, one of the lucky ones
above the surface where the real me
is bronzed in the Apollonian sun.
I stay a while, mesmerized by the glass
whose four corners frame the eyes of a man
I might have been, not liquid, not pent in.